THE OUTER BANKS & Other Poems

Other books by W. D. Ehrhart:

POETRY

A Generation of Peace, New Voices, 1975
The Awkward Silence, Northwoods Press, 1980
The Samisdat Poems, Samisdat Press, 1980
Matters of the Heart, Adastra Press, 1981
Channel Fever, Backstreet Editions, 1982
To Those Who Have Gone Home Tired: New & Selected Poems, Thunder's Mouth Press, 1984

PROSE

Vietnam-Perkasie, McFarland & Co., 1983

AS CO-EDITOR

Demilitarized Zones, East River Anthology, 1976
Those Who Were There, Dustbooks, 1984

THE OUTER BANKS & Other Poems

W. D. Ehrhart

ADASTRA PRESS
Easthampton, Massachusetts

First printing September 1984
Second printing September 1985
ISBN 0-938566-28-8

Some of these poems have appeared in *Argo*, *Asphodel*, *Friends Journal*, *The Greenfield Review*, *Many Smokes*, *Negative Capability*, *Peace or Perish*, *Piedmont Literary Review*, *Poetry East*, *Samisdat*, *Stone Country*, *Tulane Literary Magazine*, *VAFW Newsletter*, *Visions*, *Voices Israel*, the Warthog Press Broadside Series, and the 1984 *Anthology of Magazine Verse*.

ADASTRA PRESS
101 Strong Street
Easthampton, MA 01027

For my wife, Anne—
with whom I discovered the Outer Banks
and with whom I constantly rediscover,
even in a world apparently terminally mad,
the joy of living.

For Richard + Candace —
It is really wonderful
to renew an acquaintance
after all these years.
Yours
Bill
8 March 1987

CONTENTS

I.

THE DREAM

I'm at this party. We're all having fun—dancing and drinking and smoking joints, talking and laughing, bumping into each other the way you do at a party when it's very crowded and everyone is feeling loose. We're in a nice apartment, a basement apartment fixed up very modern. The livingroom is full of dancers. People are crowding around a keg in the laundryroom while others are making mixed drinks in the kitchen. The hallway is jammed with animation, dozens of conversations piling on top of each other. The bedroom is piled with coats, and there are people sitting on the coats and on the floor.

The only strange thing is the people: there's nothing wrong with them; it's just that there are friends from high school and friends from college and friends I've known from all over. They couldn't possibly all know each other or be here together like this—but here they are. Maybe it's a party for me; I don't know. Anyway, I'm having too much fun to worry about it. I feel great.

All of a sudden the door bursts open. No, it's been kicked in; it's all splintered around the latch. Eight or ten men in combat gear swagger in. They're wearing green jungle utility uniforms, flak jackets, and helmets. It's a squad of Marines. Hey, what is this?

They barge into the livingroom, knocking people out of the way with their fists and rifle butts. Wayne Gregg—I think it must be his apartment—starts for the lead man, his arms outstretched as if to say, "What are you doing?" But before he can open his mouth, the Marine opens fire full automatic with his M-16, and Wayne is blown back against the wall where he slumps down dead.

People start screaming. Other Marines are already beyond the livingroom. I can hear shouts, gunfire, and screaming coming from the back of the apartment. The Marines still in the livingroom begin shooting and bayoneting people at random. Jesus Christ! I can't believe what I'm seeing. I beg them to stop, but they don't seem to notice me. The whole place is screaming and shouting and filling up with the acrid sting of burnt gun-powder. People are trampling each other; there's nowhere to run. Mark Halley is slumped in a chair staring vaguely at his own guts which he's holding in his hands. A Marine bashes his skull in with a rifle butt. Another Marine has just climbed off Linda Titus. She's lying on the floor, naked from the waist down. He drives a bayonet through her throat and her eyes pop wide open. I can't believe it. The inside of my head feels like it's going to explode. I can't see the faces of the Marines. I keep trying to, but I can't see their faces. The apartment is full of dead and dying people now. They are lying helter-skelter everywhere, wherever they've fallen. People are whimpering and cowering in corners and behind overturned furniture, begging hysterically. Their eyes are vacant and glassy. The Marines go on shooting and stabbing. They are working methodically now, almost casually. There is blood everywhere. They don't seem to notice me at all. I don't understand why they don't shoot me. I beg them to stop.

Please, please, stop, this is insane. Mary Jane Farrell is doubled over in the hallway; she's been raped and shot in the stomach. She's crying for help. I bend down to her and try to stop the bleeding. A Marine pokes a rifle barrel past my shoulder from behind and blows the top of her head off. I scream. He doesn't even notice me. I can't understand it. Why don't they notice me?!

I run down the hall crying, but something catches my eye, and I stop abruptly. I'm standing in front of a full-length mirror. I'm dressed in combat gear. There is a black M-16 rifle in my hands. The barrel is smoking.

Please, please, stop, this is murder. Mary Jane Darnell is doubled over in the hallway, [illegible] and [illegible] the [illegible] up the back. I [illegible] down to her and try to stop the bleeding. [illegible] passes [illegible] my shoulder [illegible] the top of her head [illegible]. I scream. He doesn't even notice me. I can't understand [illegible] [illegible].

[illegible] the hall [illegible] some [illegible] [illegible] [illegible] [illegible] [illegible] [illegible] in the [illegible] hands. The barrel is smoking.

II.

II

THE FARMER

Each day I go into the fields,
to see what is growing,
and what remains to be done.
It is always the same thing: nothing
is growing; everything needs to be done.
Plow, harrow, disc, water, pray
till my bones ache and hands rub
blood-raw with honest labor—
all that grows is the slow
intransigent intensity of need.
I have sown my seed on soil
guaranteed by poverty to fail.

But I don't complain, except
to passersby who ask me why
I work such barren earth.
They would not understand me
if I stooped to lift a rock
and hold it like a child, or laughed,
or told them it is their poverty
I labor to relieve. For them,
I complain. A farmer of dreams
knows how to pretend. A farmer of dreams
knows what it means to be patient.
Each day I go into the fields.

GIFTS

for Anne Gulick Ehrhart

I give you the worst gift first
as a warning: the sullen silence
awakening in the morning; the self-
centered dolt too blunt sometimes
to button his own trousers;
the quick tongue slashing;
the perpetual anger at being
perpetually mortal.

The second gift I give you
of necessity: the come-what-may;
the kiss on the cheek on the way
out the door, real and mindless
as superstition; rumpled clothes,
broken dishes, grocery bills;
the guarantee of disagreements;
the mundane goings and comings
of daily routine.

But the third gift is a promise,
and I give it also to you: a warm
heart constantly beating;
a companion; warm arms, warm lips,
laughter brighter than mountain fire,
tears as wild as the sea;
the unrelenting desire to please;
an unrelenting struggle to know;
unrepentant exuberant love
for as long as we share this earth.

27 June 1981

CONTINUITY

Because I love my wife, I've traveled
six hundred miles to stand for fifteen minutes
by a cold stone standing in a grove of pines
in West Tisbury, Martha's Vineyard, Massachusetts.
What are you to me? A name. A few
silent photographs I've seen in albums.
Second-hand stories. I never even met you.

The taxi idles by the graveyard gate;
a cold Atlantic wind whips the pines.
Your daughter grips my arm—once, twice, hard:
"My mother died!" she cries, as though the news
had just arrived, the tears standing for a moment
in her eyes before they topple down her face.
I think of mothers, think of death, and love

and all at once my throat constricts
in startled grief; my own tears rise:
mother of my wife, your living soul
breathes in every gesture of your daughter,
and your daughter is the touchstone of my life.
Because I love my wife, I've traveled
six hundred miles to discover that I miss you,
and to thank you for the splendid child you raised.

NEW JERSEY PINE BARRENS

Sixty miles away, in New York City,
herds of cars stampede down avenues,
animated lumps of steel and fumes.
Thirty miles away, in Philadelphia,
a mugger steals a purse in broad daylight
from a screaming old woman on Broad Street.
Here, I wake to whippoorwills and bullfrogs.

Swamp cedar, scrub oak, stunted maple
whisper as I ready the canoes
beside the beaver dam on Batsto River.
The children on the school camping trip
are still asleep. A beaver tail slaps.
I urinate beside a blueberry bush,
notice white violet and lady slipper,
pickerel gliding through the quiet pond.

Soon the children will awake, all energy.
Alien and graceless in their sleek canoes,
they will spend this day ricocheting
off sunken stumps and overhanging trees,
heaping angry blame for faulty navigation
on anyone but self, their adolescent
piping shreiks splitting the awesome
silence with a day-long jagged gash.

Too young to understand, their thoughts
are all of who-rammed-who, and the hot-faced
shame of looking clumsy. I cup my hand,
dip it in the beaver pond and drink
the majesty of wilderness, wondering
how much longer will it be
before children like these will have to learn
the majesty of wilderness
from books.

PAGAN

for the people of El Salvador

In the heart of the night
that beats in the heart of the people,
something is waking
out of the half-sleep
of centuries.
Beckoned alive
by the endless nightmare of priests,
viceroys and chains,
the pestilence of toil
and submission,
where nothing has ever been sacred
but gold,
greed,
and the lash,
it rears its slow black head
and blinks its eyes open.
Its wings unfold
like the slow seepage of blood
from a festering wound:
thunder and clouds
are among the stars.
Slowly it rises
on the rising wind,
the hard white tips
of its fangs
catching the moon.

A WARNING TO MY STUDENTS

George School
November 1981

The B-1 bomber
is going to be built
after all: not scrapped, after all
our resistance; just postponed.
"Necessity requires...,"
yet another president insists;
the Secretary of State discusses
limited nuclear war
as if it were sane;
and in El Salvador, another
petty upper-class junta
needs American aid
to fight the communists.

What happened
to the last twenty years?

If I were young again,
I could do it all
differently: go to college,
go to Canada, live underground
on the lam in basement apartments
in strange cities—anything
but kill
somebody else's enemies
for somebody else's reasons.

And now I see it all
coming
one more time; one
by one, all the old flags
resurrected
and ready

for the rockets' red glare
still another time—
and I wake up nights, afraid,
and I have to reach out
and touch my wife,
just to make sure.

Sometimes she wakes up, too.
"It's all right," she says;
she strokes my head;
"It's just a dream."

And she's right, too:
these days, for me
it's just a dream

because the next time they come looking
for soldiers, they won't come looking
for me. I'm too old;
I know too much.

The next time they come looking
for soldiers, they'll come looking
for you.

SOUND ADVICE

Remember the time Jerry Doughty
beat you up for no good reason
on the ice at Sellersville while all
the other kids stood around and laughed?
You skated home alone that day, swearing
you would find a way to even up the score.
But you never did: years passed,
he moved away, your adolescent pride
still tucked beneath his belt like a trophy.

Or one year later, in the fifth grade,
when Margie Strawser told the teacher
you had hit her with a bean-shooter?
Nothing you protested mattered:
the shooter and the beans were in your desk.
You got paddled as the whole class watched,
and Margie got an A in social studies.

You should have learned something
growing up. Instead, you volunteered.
And when you found your war as rotten
as the rotting corpses of the dead
peasants lying in the green rice
they would never harvest, you were shocked
that nothing you protested mattered.
Thirteen years have passed since then,
and still your anger rises at the way people
turn away from what you have to say.

Who taught you to believe in words?
Listen: injustice is a fact.
Like dust rising when the wind blows.
Like heat when the fire rises.

A natural thing. The white space
between the lines of every history
book you've ever read. The back side
of the Golden Rule. The one unbroken law.

And yet you've quit half a dozen jobs
on principle: point of order! Point of order—
as though you think it matters more than bread.
Everywhere you go, the blade of your contempt
draws blood. No wonder people hate you.
Listen, friend: don't make us so uncomfortable.
We don't like it any more than you do,
but the world is what it is. You can't change it.
Face it. Learn to bend. We have.

SURVIVING THE BOMB ONE MORE DAY

For three days, iron cold gripped
the earth in a blue fist:
mucus froze in nostrils; lungs
ached with the weight of breathing;
cheeks turned red with pain.

Is this how we would finally end?
Not in fire; not consumed
in mushroom orange heat,
but laid out stiff and hard
like fish in a peddler's cart?

After all those nights of waking up
to thunder, sweating, thinking, "Christ,
we've finally done it," and waiting
in the eerie fog of half-awake
for the final slap of the blast.

On the third day, it began to snow.
Into the night the snow fell,
and by morning the earth was white.

But by afternoon, the wind
was tailing off, and a warming sun
foretold another night
of waiting for the fire.

EVERETT DIRKSEN,
HIS WIFE, YOU & ME

I read once that Everett Dirksen,
United States Senator, never slept
a night without his wife of fifty years.
One can almost see them, near the end:
two doddering old white-haired giggling
lovers climbing into bed, the undimmed
passion still glowing steadily from within—
enough to light the darkness one more night.

And yet I think that light was raised
against a darker darkness both, perhaps,
saw approaching years before the end.
I see it coming, too – saw it years
before I met you; it scared me then,
and still does, and you're the only one
who's ever made me feel the weight
a little less. We giggle, too, sometimes.

One might marvel at the long-enduring
passion of that husband and his wife:
fifty years without a night alone;
marvelous, indeed—
but it's other couples who amaze me:
their ignorance, their faith, their sheer
bravado. Whether we shall be together
or alone in death, I have no way of knowing;

but I know the weight, and how it feels
to pass the night without you.

COWGIRLS, TEACHERS & DREAMS

for Betsy in Montana

That day we fished Coyote Creek
from Pete's ranch to the upper barn,
dry pale prairie grass rippled
pastures mile on mile to mountains
shouldering sky. Cattle grazed the high
plateaus where men in winter still
go mad from loneliness and snow. Hard
land, its beauty self-composed; a long
way from anywhere. We shared one rod.
You showed me where the best spots were,
parted bushes—"Shhh," you said, "don't
scare the fish"—coached my clumsy casts.
It didn't help: you caught twenty; I
caught none. It didn't matter. Seven
hours working up the creek through
morning into afternoon toward evening.
Words passed softly back and forth
like dry prairie grass in wind. Magic
how that hot dry day in summer in Montana
passed so gently. At the upper barn,
we cleaned the fish: you deftly lopped
off heads and tails; taught me how
to slit their bellies, poke my finger
down the spines to clear the guts in one
swift stroke. How was I to tell you
I was squeamish? Biting flesh inside
my mouth, I did as I was shown. "It's late,"
you said, "we'd better take the horse."
How was I to tell you I was scared
of horses, hadn't ridden since that day
when I was ten and rode four wild miles
on a horse that wasn't stable-broken?
I climbed up behind you: no saddle,

nothing but your slender waist to hold—
a stalk of prairie grass in wind—and you
went straight for every ditch you saw,
jumping, laughing: "Hang on tight!"—stopping
only when you saw the mother antelope
and fauns, babies still with spots, all
three staring, undecided. Maybe next time
bobcats or wolves instead of riders.
The cook got fired while we fished.
Drinking on the job. A hard life in Big
Sky Country. I was only passing through;
I've never seen you since. Not that I
would have a reason: you were eight, and I
was twenty-two. The friends I stopped
to see were only summer help—married now,
a lawyer and a teacher in the East.
I'm a teacher, too. So were you.
And in my mind, you'll always catch
the fattest trout and ride the swiftest
horse, always stop to gaze at fauns,
and never lose your innocence or courage
in that lonely hard land you offered
to a stranger like a treasure,
like a blessing.

"...the light that cannot fade..."

Suzie, you picked a hell of a time
to teach me about mortality.
I was in North Carolina then,
talking tough, eating from cans,
wearing my helmet John Wayne style—
and you were suddenly dead:
a crushed skull on a pre-dawn road
just two weeks shy of college,
and me about to leave for Vietnam.

I wanted you and me alive;
I wanted out.
That night I cried till dawn.

Funny, how I managed to survive
that war, how the years have passed,
how I'm thirty-four and getting on,
and how your death
bestowed upon my life a permanence
I never would have had
if you had lived:

you'd have gone to college,
married some good man from Illinois,
and disappeared like all the other
friends I had back then who meant
so much and whom I haven't
thought about in years.

But as it is, I think of you
whenever dancers flow across a stage
or graceful gymnasts balance on the beam.
And every time I think of you,
you're young.

(for Carolyn Sue Brenner, 1948–1966)

CLIMBING TO HEAVEN

for Brady Shea

That evening you and I and Daniel
climbed to the peak of a barn
on a soybean farm in Payne, Ohio,
only pride compelled me
not to climb back down.

"God, this land is flat!" you shouted,
standing up abruptly, six-foot frame
astride the peak as if to climb
still higher. "Sit down," I said,
"You make me nervous." You laughed,
but out of kindness sat back down.

"See those lights?" you asked.
"Fort Wayne. Thirty miles away,
and not a thing between us
higher than a railroad overpass."

How trapped you must have felt
in Payne, Ohio.

Later I heard you'd gone to Idaho.

Later still, Daniel's letter
said you fell from a mountain in Colorado—
but I know you must have reached the peak
and climbed straight up from there.

RESPONSIBILITY

The Congress shall have power to lay and collect taxes...to...provide for the common defense and general welfare of the United States.

—Art. I, Sec. 8, Para. 1
U. S. Constitution

The sun taps on the kitchen table;
coffee boils. As birds awaken
trees beyond the window, I think of you
upstairs: your naked body curled
around a pillow, your gentle face
an easy dream of last night's love.
It's Friday; summer.

Somewhere
in another country to the south,
government troops are stalking
through a nightmare; a naked body
in the dusty street behind them
sprawls in rubbish, and a woman
in a house with the door kicked in
pounds fists on empty walls. There,
the news is always bad, the soldiers
always armed, the people
always waiting for the sound
of boots splintering wood.

What if you and I were wrenched from sleep
by soldiers, and they dragged me out
and shot me? Just like that; just
the way it happens every day:
the life we share,
all the years ahead we savor
like the rich taste of good imported coffee,
vanished
in a single bloody hole between the eyes.

Would you fix the door and go on living?
Or would the soldiers rape and shoot you, too?
Idle thoughts. Things like that don't happen
in America. The sun climbs;
the coffee's gone; time to leave for work.
Friday, payday, security:
money in my pocket for the weekend;
money for the government;
money for the soldiers of El Salvador,
two hundred bullets to the box.

THE BLIZZARD OF SIXTY-SIX

Snow came early here, and hard:
roads treacherous; wires down.
School authorities should have cancelled
the annual high school Christmas dance:
two couples died on the way home.
"Tragedy," the local papers declared,
but the snow kept falling.

Somewhere in a folder in a file
is a photograph of me in a uniform:
one stripe for PFC; girl in a yellow gown.
I took her home through the falling snow,
kissed goodnight, and left for Asia.

All through that long year, snow
fell and fell on the green rice,
on gray buffalo, thatched huts, green
patrols, and the mounting yellow dead.

Randy, class of '65, died
in terminal cold in the Mekong Delta;
Kenny, class of '66, died in a blizzard
of lead in the Central Highlands;
I came home with permanent chills,
the yellow nameless dead of Asia
crammed into my seabag, and all of us
looking for a reason.

We never found one. Presidents
come and go away like snowdrifts
in driveways; generals come and go;
the earth goes on silently turning
and turning through its seasons,
and the snow keeps falling.

CANOEING THE POTOMAC

As rivers go, this one isn't much.
It doesn't drain a continent; it doesn't
flow through wilderness; it isn't wild,
or wide, or deep. Between Antietam
and the Shenandoah, only scattered
mild rapids interrupt its calm.
What makes this river awesome
is its sadness: along these gentle
tree-lined banks, in 1861, a nation
shattered like a brittle stone.

Up ahead, at Harpers Ferry, abolitionist
John Brown captures the federal arsenal
for freedom, but he in turn is captured
by a West Point colonel, Robert E. Lee.
Behind us, nearly three years later,
Lee's Confederate Grays are met
by George McClellan's Union Blues.
Cannon shot and bugles blare
the ranks of razored bayonets across
the fields littered with the cost
of John Brown's Glory.

The Union was preserved, of course,
but the sadness remains. Our sleek
canoes move in silence through the gap
between the violence of those years
and the violence we've inherited.
Moral people, principled and kind as Lee,
still apply their talents to the sword,

and people mad as John Brown still insist
their service to the noblest ends.
Saddest of all, Browns and Blacks, Blues, Grays,
Yellows, Reds and Whites are still in chains
that bind us to the deadly past
out of which we seem this summer day
to glide with such apparent ease.

THE VISION

It can happen anywhere:
on a bus, on the street,
on a soft afternoon standing
by an old spring the first Maryland
Quakers quenched their thirst at
after a hard day in the fields;
at work—often at work—in the midst
of the dull ache of moving
from day to day; over a beer;
in the arms of the person you love.

Maybe a flower will trigger it off—
its fiery petals, yellow and orange,
dancing the breeze like cobweb;
or a girl's shy smile and hesitant
sparkling eyes; an aroma
that conjures a memory;
or the snatch of a song,
or a touch, or a word, or silence—

and the heart leaps up
like the first glimpse of the cloudless
moonless night sky above New Mexico,
and you suddenly stare
into the infinite power
of how things could be
if the dreams you live on
came true.

Only a flash,
a single terrible instant,
lifting and swift as lightening,
an explosion of joy—

and then it is gone,
and only the vision remains.

And the longing.

III.

THE OUTER BANKS

1.

Hysterical seagulls dart and soar
through evening's rising calm. Some alight,
and strut like tiny generals among the children
chasing spindly ghost crabs on the beach.
Here, a fisherman. There, two lovers sharing secrets.
And there a kite, riding a stiff sea breeze
that makes the dune grass ripple and toss
like slow green rollers just before they burst,
exploding phosphorescent white on dark wet sand.
A half-mile south, Cape Hatteras light, its tower
spiraled black and white, begins to flash
in deepening twilight. Stars appear.
Beachfires rise and flicker.
The flash atop Cape Hatteras light becomes a soft
revolving beam casting silver light on rooftops,
dune tops, sand and surf, then skittering over waves
and out to sea.
Returning.
Gone again.
And back.
And gone.
A perpetual circle of moving light.
An all-night silent song.

2.

Here, between Cape Henry and Cape Fear,
the Gulf Stream and the Labrador Current
collide: the turbulence of opposites,
the centuries of wind and tide
have built the Outer Banks,
a slender stalk of weathered land,
two hundred narrow miles of low-slung sand
between deep water and the Carolina coast.
Behind them lie the sounds: Currituck
and Albemarle, Pamlico and Core:
rippling sheets of shallow pale green.
To seaward lie the shoals: Wimble, Diamond,
Frying Pan and Lookout: restless nightmares
shifting, ever shifting, like the tentacles
of an octopus, like grinding dragons' teeth.
Exposed, and hunched against the seasons,
the banks are shifting, too:
northeasters scrape the beaches raw;
gales uproot what little that remains of forests;
hurricanes tear gaping holes from sea to sound,
and overnight, grain by infinite grain,
old inlets disappear; roads and houses
disappear, docks, dunes, ponds and marshes.
Wind on sand, sea on sand, sand on sand;
a thousand years, five thousand years:
still the banks endure.

3.

Verrazano thought the banks an isthmus;
the sounds beyond, the legendary oriental sea.
Amadas and Barlowe, sailing under Raleigh,
claimed the banks for England and the Queen.
"The people of the countrey," Barlowe wrote,
"are very handsome, and a goodly people,
in their behavior mannerly, and civill,
gentle, loving, void of guile and treason."
Croatoans on the banks; along the sounds,
Poteskeets and Machapungas, Woccons,
Neuse and Corees: fisherpeople, gatherers
of wild grapes and melons, deer hunters.
"I think in all the world," wrote Barlowe,
"the like aboundance is not to be found."
Elizabeth, impressed, issued Letters Patent.
Three successive settlements on Roanoke failed—
the last, shrouded in mysterious disaster.
Still the English dreamed, and finally,
further north, Jamestown closed the cover
on the ancient book of tribes,
and wrote the names of Indians on maps.

4.

Milestones:

Virginia Dare born at Roanoke, 1587.

First permanent English settlement on the banks, 1664.

Blackbeard killed and beheaded at Ocracoke, 1718.

First public tavern on the banks, 1757.

Profession of pilot closed to Blacks, 1773.

First U. S. Marines on the banks, 1778.

First lighthouse on the Carolina coast, Cape Fear, 1783.

Last known reference to Native Americans on the banks, 1788.

First attempt to mark Diamond Shoals fails, 1823.

Steamer *Home*, carrying 135 passengers and two life-jackets, wrecked off Hatteras with the loss of 90 lives, 1837.

Whaling gun introduced to the banks, 1875.

Rasmus Midgett, unassisted, rescues all ten people from the barkentine *Priscilla* during a hurricane, 1899.

Orville Wright: "We came down here for wind and sand, and we have got them;" Kitty Hawk, 1900.

Audubon Society gains protection for egrets and terns, nearly extinct by the turn of the century, 1903.

First paved highway on the banks, 18 miles, 1931.

The Lost Colony first performed at Roanoke, 1937.

5.

From the sounds and inlets of the Outer Banks,
nimble
English privateers raided Spanish treasure fleets.
Later came the runaways and fugitives:
indentured servants, Africans and outlaws,
pirates from the Caribbean, shipwrecked seamen.
Some came and went; others stayed
beyond the reach of warrants, writs, and masters.
Cold to strangers, clannish, making do with two-room
shacks in sheltered sound-side woods and marshes,
those early Bankers hunted, fished and farmed
survival, combing beaches in the wake of storms,
stripping stranded ships for salvage,
rendering the carcasses of whales: rooting,
clinging, holding on like stubborn dune grass.
Scarbroughs, Midgetts, Gaskills, Dixons, Grays.
Names on gravestones; names on the rolls
of the lighthouse keepers and surfboat rescue crews;
names on tackle shops, restaurants, homes and stores:
children and children of children's children
live and grow old and bequeath to their children
the will to adapt to a shifting world
defined by weather, sand, and tides.

6.

Sea bass, striped bass, bluefish and butter fish,
carp and croakers, eel, herring,
Spanish mackerel, menhaden and mullet,
shad, sharks, spot and sturgeon,
northern and southern weakfish,
clams, crabs, oysters, scallops and shrimp;
porpoises and whales;
diamondback terrapin and loggerhead turtles.

7.

Near rushes in a marshy pond in Buxton Woods,
an egret, like a solomn elder of the realm,
stands alone knee-deep in water. The posture
of the bird suggests a kind of wisdom,
or a perfect inner calm. Behind the bird,
beyond the woods, the black and white spiral
of the lighthouse rises. Bird and lighthouse;
blue sky; the silence of the whispered afternoon.
An old road, a rutted double sand-track
long overgrown, passes by the pond and disappears
through loblolly pines toward old abandoned houses.
A bare breath of wind disturbs the rushes:
the black beak turns; the stilt-like legs
take two steps forward; the slow broad wings
unfold. The great bird flies.

8.

Stand on the beach at night at Cape Hatteras
looking east across the water. Keep watching:
there!   Flash.   Flash.
That's the beacon on the Texas Tower
marking the outer edge of Diamond Shoals.

The buoys placed on Diamond Shoals
washed away in a storm.
The lightship stationed on the shoals
broke loose and wrecked in a storm.
The floating bell beacon disappeared.
More buoys washed away.
The Diamond Shoals lighthouse project
ended in a storm before completion.
Another lightship stationed on the shoals
broke loose and wrecked in a storm.
A German U-boat sank another.

Look again at the flashing light.
Look at the darkness between the flashes.
Look at the waiting sea.

9.

Barks and barkentines,
brigs and brigantines,
battleships, barges and yachts;
flyboats and pilot boats,
gunboats and fishing boats,
ironclads, trawlers and tugs;
transports and tankers,
surfboats and schooners,
submarines, steamers and sloops;
liners and lightships,
cutters and clipperships
broken and wrecked on the banks.

10.

The sea breeze gently rubs the dunes. The sky
is clear. The beach is empty now of children,
fishers, fires, and kites. Only the lovers,
huddled down for shelter in the hollow of a dune,
stay to watch the light revolving, listening
to its song. What secrets do they share
as night moves on toward dawn? Ageless secrets.
Timeless secrets. Listen to their muffled giggles
drifting on the air. This is how it always is
because all lovers think themselves
immortal. How else could we go on?
Cape Hatteras light casts silver light on rooftops,
dunetops, sand and surf, skittering over waves
and out to sea.
Returning.
Gone again.
And back.
And gone.

ABOUT THE AUTHOR

W. D. Ehrhart was born in 1948 and grew up in Perkasie, Pennsylvania. He holds degrees from Swarthmore College and the University of Illinois at Chicago Circle. He currently lives in Doylestown, PA with his wife, Anne. His work has appeared in *The Virginia Quarterly Review*, *TriQuarterly*, *New Letters*, *The Chronicle of Higher Education*, *From A to Z: 200 Contemporary American Poets*, and *Leaving the Bough: 50 American Poets of the 80s*. He has received awards and grants from The Academy of American Poets, the University of Illinois, The Mary Roberts Rinehart Foundation and the Pennsylvania Council on the Arts. Ehrhart is one of only two poets represented in *Vietnam: An Anthology and Guide to a Television History*.

The first printing was handset in Garamond Old Style types, printed handfed letterpress, sewn by hand, bound in a paperback edition of 275, with 25 copies in cloth over board, signed and numbered by the author. The second printing is perfect bound, offset printed, with photo-plates made from the original proofs corrected for this printing. Covers for both editions were letterpress printed, the first having three colors and the second, two. Editorial and production offices at:
Adastra Press, 101 Strong St, Easthampton, MA 01027